Care, Duck & Weave

A story written by
Zoe Harvey about being
a Youth Care Worker.

Zoe Harvey

Strategic Book Publishing and Rights Co.

Strategic Book Publishing and Rights Co.
12620 FM 1960, Suite A4-507
Houston, TX 77065
www.sbpra.com

ISBN: 978-1-62516-276-2

This story is dedicated to the wonderful young people I have had the pleasure of working with since I first became a youth worker.

I am proud of you all. You have shown growth, integrity, charm, and manners, and the ability to deal with past issues, move on, and make something of your lives.

CONTENTS

Chapter 1
The Beginning of
a Rewarding Career Move

When I was seventeen, I started out working as a dental nurse, a career that lasted over twenty years and taught me a great deal about the emotions of human beings in pain. Then I decided it was time for a change and worked in the hospitality industry for five years. During that time, I became a counsellor and learned much about the general public's troubles, trials, and tribulations. This gave me even more insight into human emotions. After five years in hospitality, I changed careers and started working in Job Network. This entailed working with people from all walks of life. Once again, I learned more about human emotions and the troubles people faced in society.

It was at this point that I decided to get into my dream job of becoming a youth worker. While working full time at Job Network I went back to school—something I hadn't done in a very long time. This venture seemed quite daunting at first, as I had decided to study externally whilst working. This meant many evenings and early mornings reading, researching online, and completing assignments. I am proud to say that I completed my Diploma of Youth Work ahead of schedule and attended my graduation ceremony at the Brolga Theatre in Maryborough in 2010. I was fifty-three years old. I was so proud and grateful to have been given the chance to enhance my knowledge and enter the field I had dreamed of for so many years. Having said this, I also really needed the other life experiences behind me to be able to be successful as a youth worker. It was a great moment to stand in front of other students, their families, and some of my own family to accept my Diploma Certificate.

Now came the challenge: to become employed in the youth care industry without specific experience in this area. I drew upon my experiences in job services working with troubled youth and adults who were less fortunate than most of us. There were teen pregnancies, homeless youth, youth from non-supportive families, youth and adults at risk of homelessness, and the biggest challenge of all: youth and adults who showed signs of suicidal ideation.

I rely a great deal on gut instinct, and it has rarely let me down. Fortunately, I had an employer who believed in my ability to help people, even though sometimes

I could have been proven wrong. He was a marvellous mentor for me and backed my intuition when I was convinced that a client was in danger. Some of the gut instincts that come to mind were quite mind-blowing, but most resulted in successful outcomes. I shall describe some of these instances, and then you may see how my gut instinct kicked in and was correct. Of course, I used facts as well, but sometimes things are not what you see as fact. Sometimes you have to go on inner feelings.

One young man that was on my caseload had no direction in life; all he wanted to do was party all night and sleep during the day. I asked this young man if he had any ambitions in life, and he responded: "If you need an ambition in life, then your life is crap. I live the way I do because I don't think I will be alive at twenty-five."

His response shocked me initially, but then it made me look deeper into what made this young man function as he did. This young man was seventeen years old, so it was tragic that he felt this way. He came to appointments very unwillingly and often did not show up; however, I pursued his appointment schedule until he finally started coming to all our appointments. I think the fact that I just sat and listened to this young man was the turning point for him. My job was to try and engage him in education or work; but I felt that if I did not take the time to listen and understand him, I would be setting him up to fail—which would be very detrimental to his well-being. As the young man attended more appointments, he opened up and the conversations grew longer. I could see an extremely intelligent, yet troubled, young man before me. I had the ability to refer clients to be assessed, and I had done so twice. Both times the assessor sent him back to my caseload. This disturbed me, as I had the inner feeling something was still not right.

After my contract at that job ended, I left. Later, I read in the newspaper that this young man had been involved in serious violence and would serve a prison sentence. It made me sad and angry, as I had known something was wrong and no one would listen to me.

I had the pleasure of working with a female client who had been on someone else's caseload. I had asked to take her on as a client when she came into the office very distressed one day. No one had ever taken her seriously, and, once again, my inner feelings suggested that something serious was happening to this woman. We talked for over an hour. She cried and told me how she was feeling and that she wanted to come and see me the next day because she trusted me. We made the appointment, and the woman arrived early the following day. Alarm bells were ringing by this time, as she looked like someone who had totally lost her way. I immediately got in touch with the on-site assessor, who didn't have time to see the woman until later that day. I asked her to come into my office, which was not sterile with blank walls, but instead plastered with colourful positive sayings. I managed to get my client to stay; however, she wanted me to attend the assessment with her. As I said earlier, my employer was an understanding person and allowed me to do this for my client. I had seen this woman go from a confident, healthy woman earlier in the year to a frail and very troubled person now. An appointment was made immediately at the local mental health clinic. I attended this appointment with the client and was shocked at what was going on in her life; I had only been told the tip of the iceberg. Later, I was allowed to drive her home.

This woman's case was ultimately a success story—after many long counselling sessions, a change in residence, and many appointments with me. I am happy to report that she is now leading a whole, rewarding life. I hope she will never look back.

I worked with another woman in a similar position; no one had faith in her. This lady was highly educated in another country, yet her qualifications were not recognised in Australia. She was highly intelligent, but she had sustained post-traumatic stress disorder (PTSD) many years before and was still suffering to a degree.

You can learn a great deal from listening and watching body language. I listened to this woman and learned about her inner traumas and thoughts just by observing. We had many, many appointments, and eventually she found a part-time position in her area of her expertise. Although the position was technically part time, it ended up being more like full time thanks to the hours she spent writing reports. This woman was very dedicated to her job and showed great promise. The company she worked for, however, wanted more and more from her without offering extra remuneration, and she eventually resigned when the workload became too much for her. Although this woman was not shy when it came to hard work and working by the book, she was feeling pressured and her work was not as thorough as usual. After she left this demanding job, she started working closer to her home as a kitchen hand and was most successful in this position, working extremely hard and long hours. This employment ended when the restaurant changed managers and employed a completely new staff.

This is yet another success story, as this woman has just released the first book of a trilogy on Amazon. I have had the pleasure of reading the book, and she captures readers from the very beginning, enabling them to visualise and be part of the story. I cannot name names in my book, but you know who you are. Congratulations, and keep doing what you are doing—moving onwards and upwards.

I have many more stories to tell of those less fortunate, but I will continue on to my dream job. I still wonder how my old clients are doing and often bump into them at the shops. When I do, we say hello and have a chat.

From this point I applied for a position as a youth worker and was hired straight away in residential care. My dream was coming true at long last. But as I said earlier, this would not be an easy job without life experience, and even then it could be mentally demanding—yet most rewarding.

Caring, helping, listening, being there for all people

Chapter 2
Youth Work Begins in the Residential

A Guide to the Qualities You Need

Being a youth worker can be challenging, demanding, and dangerous, but it can also be most rewarding. Every time you see a positive, you will feel like you have won the lottery—and, believe me, that feeling is more than magic.

The most important part of being a youth worker is having an open mind and realising that if the children in care were from regular families, they would not be in residential care. You cannot compare "normal" children and those who are in residential care. I hate the word "normal," but some people perceive certain behaviours as normal and other behaviours as abnormal—part of our judgmental society. If you make this comparison, you will be destined not only to fail, but also to do more harm than good in the children's lives. This will also make your job extremely difficult and the ability to make positive changes impossible.

Listening to and observing the children is imperative

if you want to understand their personalities and how they may react. I say *may* react because when you think you can read how a traumatised child will react, he or she will throw you a curveball that you have not experienced before. It is a job that is in constant flux.

Study the child's background from information issued by children's services. Even when you read the information provided, however, it will only be the tip of the iceberg. It can be horrendous reading, and you will question human beings and their behaviours, but it does happen more often than we realise. We are here to help these children, be there for them for 24/7, and encourage gradual, positive change. Most days there will be no change, but keep trying.

Life experience can help you do the work you have chosen, as you can draw on these experiences to assist the children under your care. Be professional and, most importantly, do not judge.

You need to be open to change, open to outbursts, open to being sworn at, and able not to take any of the children's behaviours personally; their outbursts usually stem from frustration or painful memories rearing their ugly heads. When the children express themselves with outbursts, this is usually a coping mechanism that they have used their whole lives; they do not know any different. There is an old saying: Change does not happen overnight. Children may be a particular age, but this does not mean they are developmentally or cognitively that age, so you must also take this into account. Sometimes the cognitive age has not been assessed. These children do not see themselves in the way you think they should; and this is due to their pasts. You need to have great patience, and I cannot say it often enough: LISTEN and OBSERVE. These will be great learning mechanisms for you.

Another imperative in this industry is—CONSISTENCY. When working in a residential setting, you will be working with a team of youth workers on different shifts. You need to be part of a team that works towards a common goal, and consistency is the key. Every worker works in a different way; however, you can work independently and still be consistent. In a residential, children thrive on consistency and boundaries, things they have never experienced before. However, it takes time for them to accept these two things, as they are foreign to them. Once consistency and boundaries are in place and accepted, the children will react badly if they are not in place because their uncertain world has changed once again.

These children—and most other people—do not adapt easily to change. Implement change slowly, one thing at a time, and ensure that it is explained thoroughly to the children. Create a visual chart of the change so that the children can see what is happening in their world.

Have you heard parents say "I have eyes in the back of my head"? Well, in youth work you need not only eyes in the back of your head, but two sets of ears as well! Children think they have invented a new "naughty" thing every day; they cannot comprehend that most adults have already done it or at least thought of it. Sometimes, when the children get into mischief they think they have invented, you will feel as if you have "I am stupid" tattooed on your forehead. Children tend to think of adults as an old dinosaurs from time beginning, too old to have experienced anything relevant to them.

You will be told many times, "You are just working for the money and you don't really care." Personally, I would like a dollar for every time has said this to me; I would be a rich woman indeed. When a child says this to you, just keep reiterating, "I am here because I care." This will fall mostly on deaf ears, particularly during an incident; however, if you truly mean it and keep saying it, the young people you care for will eventually believe it.

You will also hear, "The other youth workers let us . . ." Stick to your instincts and your job's guidelines and you will figure out that the little cherubs are just trying to get their own way—or divide and conquer the staff. Remember that the children you are looking after can be very clever and persuasive, as this is how they have had to survive in the world they came from.

Always leave your personal life at home when you walk in the door for work. The children can sense how you are feeling, sometimes even before you know yourself. Once again, these children have had to be perceptive to survive.

Yelling and screaming are another survival mechanism for these children, as this is what they have learned from their natural family environment. Sometimes they throw objects to get attention and property damage occurs. It is not a good way to get attention, but it has worked for them in the past or they have seen parents do it—a learned behaviour. Most of the behaviour is trauma-based: Horrendous things have happened to these children in the past, and these things can trigger behaviours. It could be as simple as the smell of a certain perfume, a particular colour you wear, or perhaps a facial feature that reminds the children of someone in their past.

When you have your first shift with new children, they will most likely try and work you out as soon as possible. Sometimes this will mean giving you a hard time. Children in care often do this to see if you will stay, because in the past people they care about have left them. You can see why they are suspicious of new people; they are probably thinking, "Here we go again—someone who says they care and will be gone in a week." The young ones will most likely push every button you have to push to see how you will react. My advice is to remain calm, and do not take anything said or done personally. This can sometimes be extremely hard, depending on your mood; this is why it is best to come on shift having left any issues from outside work at the gate.

When young people are experiencing anxieties, frustration, not getting their own way, or not even knowing why they are angry, it's better to let them vent their emotions. Then, when they have calmed down, see if you can work out a better way to deal with problems together. Because some children blank out their pasts and are not always cognitively able to understand their emotions, they may not even know what the emotion is called or what they are feeling—e.g., sad, angry, nervous, etc. These emotions will most likely need to be explained to the children over time by asking pertinent questions: *What do you feel when you are angry? Give examples of tightness in the stomach or chest, or any other symptoms.*

Being a good communicator helps you in your job in many ways. Communication with the children should be clear and concise to ensure the children understand what you are saying. Because you are part of a team that works together, it is imperative to keep communication lines open. At the beginning and end of each shift, you will have a changeover period when staff going off shift and those coming on can discuss what has happened that day or evening. Being part of a team means feeling comfortable talking to each other openly. If you are on shift together and you disagree with a decision; under no circumstances should you talk about this in front of the children. Take the matter up with your co-worker in private, as sometimes one of you may not have understood why something was done, or you may feel that it showed good judgment. When an incident occurs, it is best to discuss the actions taken with your co-worker, to dissect the occurrence, and to see if it was handled to the best of your ability—or if there could have been more positive outcomes.

One thing you must never, ever do is talk disparagingly about the children's parents or relatives. No matter what has happened in a child's past with family, remember that they are family and that the children do love them—even if they have been mistreated. Parents can never be replaced; however, youth workers can become surrogate parents once they have built a rapport with the children and gained their trust.

dandelion
5/12/12

Children often have time with family, as the main aim is generally to reunite them. Sometimes a youth worker must supervise the family visits. Other times, meetings can be pre-arranged with child safety's permission. There are more extreme cases where contact with a particular family member is not allowed at all. Visitation rights depend on why a particular child is under the banner of child services.

The keys to successful youth care work are consistency, honesty, patience, caring, a desire to be in the industry, empathy, good listening and communication skills, following direction, obeying procedures and legalities, knowing when you need a break, self-care, life experience, ability to accept constructive criticism, being a team player, the ability to stay calm and in control of your emotions in difficult situations, and constant willingness to learn new skills.

I have attended personal development courses outside working hours, and these have been invaluable experiences not only in intense learning; but in getting to know other people in my industry. One of these personal development courses addressed problem behaviour in children. Peter Marrington, who was a wealth of knowledge, instructed the course. Marrington works with troubled children every day and has used his experiences to teach others how to understand and work with problem behaviours to get the children on a better path.

The second personal development course I attended, delivered by Karen Alder, was in art therapy. This was a most enlightening day. Karen showed students how certain feelings can be brought out not through the spoken word, but instead through drawing. At one point, we had to write a small book on a success we have had with a client. This task showed how positive our work can be in baby steps.

One thing to NEVER do is to be disrespectful about the Young Person's family, because no matter what has happened in their past they love their parents. Parents can never be replaced, however, Youth Workers can become surrogate parents once you have built up a rapport and gained the trust of the Young People. I am now pursuing a diploma in Coordination and Management in Community Services to advance in my career of choice.

The circle of consistency and true caring leads to good rapport with the Young People and better chance of great outcomes for them.

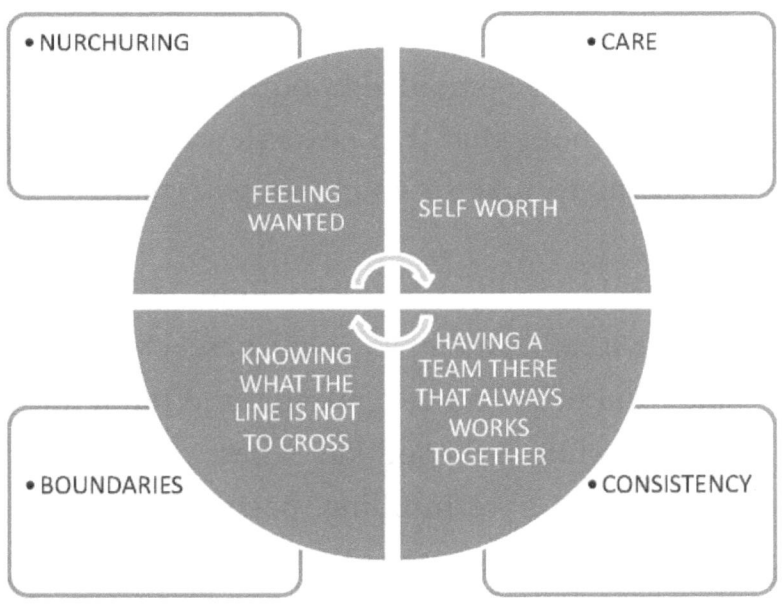

NURCHURING

CARE

FEELING WANTED

SELF WORTH

KNOWING WHAT THE LINE IS NOT TO CROSS

HAVING A TEAM THERE THAT ALWAYS WORKS TOGETHER

BOUNDARIES

CONSISTENCY

Chapter 3
My Experiences as a Youth Worker

Well, where do I begin? I have had so many experiences, both positive and negative, that it is difficult to remember them all sometimes. That said, all my experiences have provided important learning curves in my career. I hope that these experiences will also give you something to take to your own workplace.

Children display challenging behaviours at times; however, we must all remember that these children have not come from positive backgrounds, and hidden within each problem child is a good kid. These children can be turned around to have fulfilling, positive lives with the help of youth workers patient enough to assist them.

Our job is to help the children to make positive choices, and my way of achieving this is to reiterate, "Think for a couple of seconds before you do something, and it can make the difference between a good choice and a bad choice that will likely end up in trouble for you." I have said this many times. It can take some time before the words actually mean something to the children, though.

Another way to assist the children is to be honest with them. If you make a mistake, do not be afraid to say you have made a mistake or given incorrect information, as this shows the children that you are human and do not know everything. I have always told the children in my care, "I will be totally honest with you, and if I don't know something, I will find out for you." Make sure to follow up if you are asked to do something or if you do not have the answer, as this will help the children to have faith in you. If you do not follow up, the children will most likely come back at you with, "See? I knew you didn't care."

There are many behaviours that you would not expect, but that do happen in reality. I will try to explain some of these in hypothetical terms that are easily understood.

Imagine the movie *The Towering Inferno* on a miniature scale: Flames are coming under your door and you have a split second to respond to this danger. Would you move out of the way or stay where you are?

Then you may see fire elsewhere, in a scene similar to the one above, but this time on the outside of the building. In this case, you would have longer to react and, because you wouldn't feel so threatened, and you would respond quite differently.

Young people tend to want to escape when a situation gets out of hand, and they don't necessarily follow the "think for two seconds before you do anything" adage. They can end up making a wrong choice. "Absconding" is a term we use when a young person has left the residential and their whereabouts are unknown, or perhaps their whereabouts are known and the environment is not safe. When a young person absconds, youth workers have several protocols to follow. These protocols also apply to any situation where behaviours need to be logged with the child's community service officer (CSO]. Youth workers are obliged to let the on-call people know what is happening, with in-depth details about the young person—not only for the young person's safety, but to enable us to write incident reports. An incident report is a preformat that is filled in and signed by staff when a dangerous situation arises for a young person or staff member. The coordinator then read it and sends it to the Department of Child Safety to be forwarded to the young person's CSO for note and possible action. We also have to ring child safety after hours and write up a detailed report of what happened, which child safety forwards to the

CSO. This way, everyone is informed, case plans can be adjusted around behaviours, and safety plans can be implemented.

This may seem like a great deal of information, and it may be confusing when you are a new staff member. Once you have been shown how to correctly fill out an incident report, however, it is not difficult to complete.

Sometimes when children abscond, you feel like a parent whose child has just disappeared without telling you where he or she has gone. You pace and pace until the child returns. Then you are so relieved that the child is safe, but you also want to give him or her a piece of your mind. It is ok to let the young people in your care know you were worried about them, as it shows them you care (though maybe not at the time, as they usually come home hungry and just want to eat). They may not have had this response from their families—CARING. Sometimes you may even get an apology from them for absconding and sometimes not; this doesn't matter be-cause at least they know you care. Some of the young people are tough little cookies; they have had to be to survive, but you must get to the point where they hear and take in what you are saying.

Bickering is another behaviour that can either be harmless or turn into something more serious. Sometimes weapons may be used if things are not resolved. Anything can be used as a weapon, and until you are in the position of caring for troubled youth, you could not imagine the things that are used as weapons, I shall give you some examples:

» High-heeled shoes
» Household wood
» Car seat headrests
» Food in tins or jars
» Bodily fluids (e.g., spit)
» Smashed crockery
» Cutlery
» Aerosol cans
» Sharp kitchen knives (Warning: Never leave these in the house unattended, and always lock them in the staffroom.)
» Seatbelts
» Car handbrakes (which can be pulled while someone is driving)
» Pavers
» Garden implements (Lock these in a shed.)
» Broom handles
» Chairs

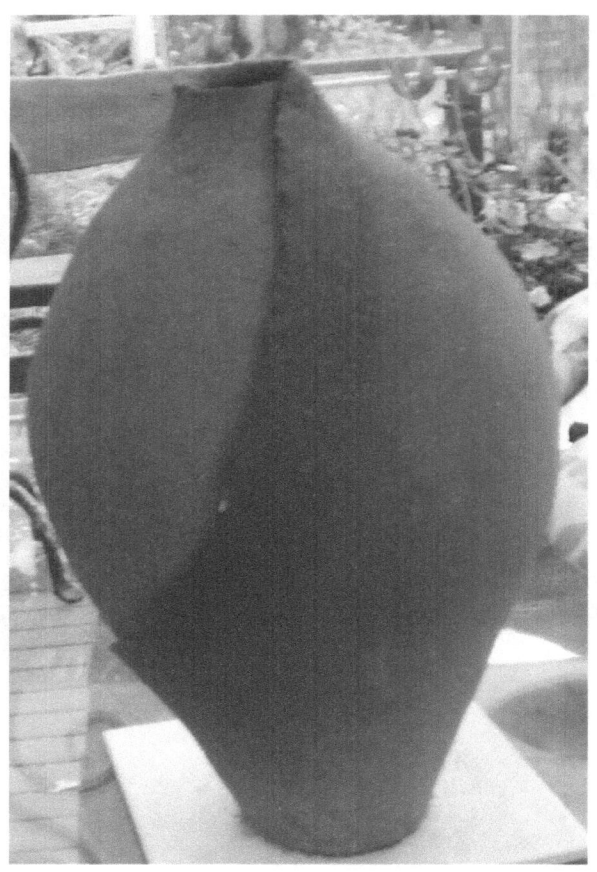

My list could go on for pages, but I'm sure you get my gist by now.

My advice to anyone new to this industry: Take a really good look at the residence and try to put yourself in an angry person's place. You will be amazed at what can become a weapon.

When a young person is heightened (angry or upset), you need to think quickly—not only for your own safety, but also for the safety of the young person(s). Listen to the Young Person, but do not put yourself in danger if there are missiles flying at you; retreat to the locked office. (This is called "planned ignoring," and it ensures safety for both parties.) Sometimes when young people are heightened, they don't even know what emotion they are feeling. It would be appropriate to compare a heightened young person to a child throwing a tantrum, as some young people lack the cognitive ability to understand that you are trying to help. We talk to the young person after an incident, when he or she has fully calmed. We discuss what the child is feeling and work out how he or she might handle the situation better next time.

Police sometimes get involved in incidents, such as self-harm and suicidal ideation cases. This is where a carer/youth worker needs to be very alert. Sometimes these young people need to be taken to hospital for assessment.

Hospital assessments can seem to take forever, particularly after you have waited a couple of hours in a cold, sterile room. In one of my cases, a young girl was assessed and the person assessing her was not sensitive enough. My client lost her desire to disclose and instead became angry and verbally inappropriate before being sent home. A golden opportunity to uncover deep emotion was lost.

We have to remember that we are not allowed to touch the young people in a residential. Even if they are fighting and you need to separate them, this is "restrictive practice" under the legal parameters of the Department of Child Safety, so use the tools you will learn to defuse the situation, such as showing concern, being alert, and planned ignoring if the situation requires it. It is a priority to ensure the safety of all involved parties, and consistency and honesty are key when working as a Youth Worker.

Sometimes there will be a hierarchy in the residence, where one young person has become the "controller" of others. This child will not accept blame for things that happen and instead will expect another child to take the blame. Youth workers can usually see this happening; however, we need to wait for the blame-taker to self-disclose that it was the other person. Then the youth workers can take action.

When you leave a residence, it can be for several reasons, such as promotion to another residence or a career change. In these cases, the young person may feel deserted once again, as he or she may have been by family members. I have experienced this myself, so I wrote the young person a letter:

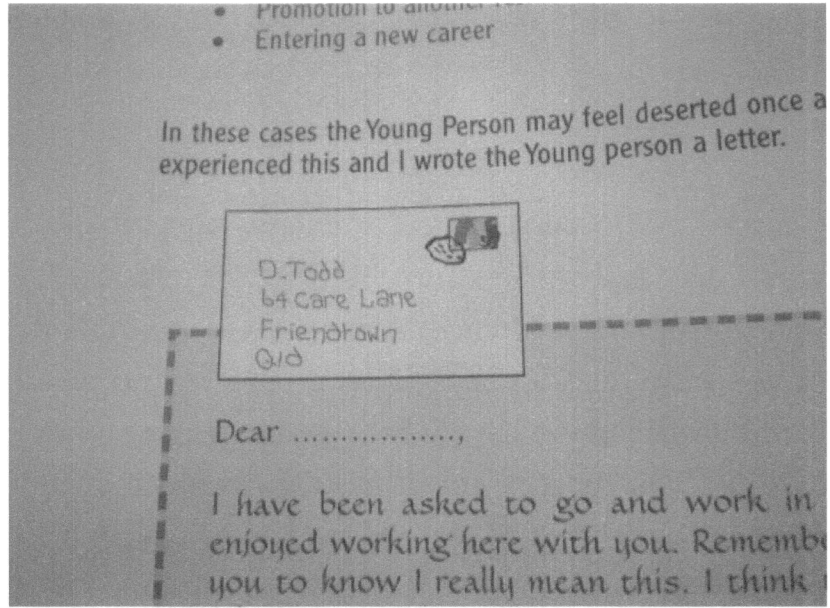

Dear ——— *,*

I have been asked to go and work in another residence. I have thoroughly enjoyed working here with you. Remember when I told you that I care about you? Well, I want you to know I really mean this. I think you have great potential and will go a long way in life. I promise to call at least once a week to see how you are. You know that when I say I'll do something, I will, so take care until I see you again. Please do not feel like I am going away, as I will visit you as long as you want me to.

Be good!

Cheers,

[Zoe]

If you promise to do something for a young person, you must carry out that promise, whether it be calling, going to a birthday dinner, or visiting. That way you do not let the child down as so many others have done in the past.

Verbal inappropriateness (i.e., abuse) can be another danger, especially when travelling in the car. It is my policy to pull over when this occurs, as it is most dangerous to drive under these circumstances and also inappropriate behaviour on the young person's part. If necessary, you can get out of the car until the outburst ends. If you are part of a team and two workers are on shift, you need to work together. If you do pull the car over, it can make a trip a very long one, especially if the young person settles and then heightens again.

Grocery shopping, a normal part of your life, can also be quite daunting. Sometimes the young person does not want to go grocery shopping, but we are trying to teach life skills. However, the young person may become heightened whilst carrying out the chore. I have had to leave trolleys full of groceries in the store and abandon shopping on several occasions when a young person has misbehaved. Here are some things that might go awry:

» Trolleys being run into people
» Knocking things off shelves
» Swearing and calling customers inappropriate names
» Being told "no" when they want something

Some young people just can't cope with the everyday things that you and I can, so it is important to pre-plan things that need to be done. Even then things can go wrong, so be prepared for the unexpected.

If you are observant as a youth worker, you can sometimes see behaviours coming. Here are some signs:

» A change in the eyes (e.g., a glazed or tunnel vision look)
» Change in facial expression or colour
» Fists clenching
» Fidgeting
» Vocal tone change

eyes are the vision into the soul....

The kitchen can be "fun," and I say that tongue in cheek place to begin an incident that will leave the house looking like a scene from the film *Cheaper by the Dozen*.

Well, where would you begin? It would be the worst mess you could encounter, and you would not even begin to know where to start cleaning, because foodstuff covers the entire house – walls, floors, ceilings, drapes, and furniture. Gobsmacked at the mess, you would walk from room to room to peruse the damage.

Hypothetically, you will probably get the gist of what you could face. You would be tempted to ring the coordinator and say, "HELP!" But you would resist until the sharp objects were removed, to ensure the safety of all present. Six a.m. came, and decided to ring the co-ordinator, whom I knew was an early riser. I mentioned to her that she might like to come to work early and peruse the new décor, and I would have an ambulance waiting for her after she had seen the sight. Now I am being flippant!

You could call it the My Kitchen/House Rules mess!

If the coordinator said to leave the mess, she would ring the area manager to come and see the mess also, before the clean up began. When you think about it, it might remind you of a Jackson Pollock painting. Perhaps you could charge admission at the front door to see the creativity of our little "cherubs" (no disrespect to Jackson Pollock). Here I go being flippant again, but you really do have to keep a sense of humour in this industry. You could also sing "Slip Slidin' Away."

Then here comes the train. Remember: "ALL ABOARD." All staff in attendance should help clean. Your shoes would never be the same after traipsing through that mess, and they would go in the trash bin, though you could save a shoe for posterity.

Chapter 4
Continual Study

I have found that, whilst working in this industry, I must continually upgrade my skills. Policies, procedures, guidelines, The Child Safety Act, and various other aspects of my role change frequently.

It is also a good idea to research external studies, to improve the following areas:

» Knowledge
» Skills
» Capabilities
» Teamwork
» Possibility for promotion
» Devising strategies to share with the team
» Talking amongst the team to improve what is not working (this is also classed as "extra learning")
» In-house training so that the company works as a unit and all residences follow the same procedures. This enables youth workers to work in other residences.

» Using staff meetings to discuss issues or strategies we have learned as a team

I have studied externally in the fields of behavioural problems and art therapy, and I am currently pursuing a Diploma in Coordination and Management in Community Services. As of 2013, I am enrolled in university to pursue a bachelor's degree in social work.

Our brains are like sponges, and the more we use them, the more we can learn and bring to the workplace. A well-run team and residence makes life much easier and more professional. We have a very difficult job, and the more we learn and work together, the easier it is.

Chapter 5
The Great Things That Happen

I have mentioned some of the challenging behaviours in previous chapters; however, many more great things happen—and when they do, you know you are doing a good job. It feels like you have won the lotto.

It's the little things, such as the young people saying:

» Thanking you
» Using your name instead of "carer"
» Not using inappropriate language when talking to you
» Asking when you are on shift again
» Saying hello when you come on shift
» Saying goodnight when you are on an overnight shift
» Asking if you want help with something you are doing
» Young people that have left the service sending messages to keep in touch after they have moved away from the district

The things they do:

» Have respect for themselves and for you
» Smile, along with the dimples in their cheeks and sparkles in their eyes
» Behave like children playing
» Laugh
» Have conversations
» Feel comfortable enough to divulge issues from their past
» Want to help with cooking and other chores
» Want to participate in activities planned for them
» Show concern for staff

The things they achieve:

» Independent living skills
» Social skills
» Budgeting when grocery shopping
» Going to school
» Commencing courses
» The ability to live with other residents in the home and get along well
» The ability to work situations out by themselves
» The ability to ask for help to solve problems
» Positive interaction with family members

All of the above things are positives in the young person's life, and these achievements demand high praise, as this builds self-esteem. Self-esteem is a huge step for these children, as it has not been present in their past. It enables them to move forward in a positive way.

Each little step—and they are baby steps—is such a thrill to the team of youth workers. It shows that the young people trust you to teach them something.

Can you remember a time at work when someone praised you for doing something well? How did you feel? I bet you felt proud of yourself. Well, it is no different for the young people; they need attention for the good things they do, which encourages a snowball effect of more good to come. Of course, you may see some inappropriate behaviour in between, but with praise they try harder to do well.

Consistency leads to trust, which leads to children feeling safe and wanting to do good things; after all, trust and safety are paramount in their lives.

Although I have only listed the good things, you can probably imagine how you and the young person feel. Even when things get ugly, try and see the bright side; the ugly stuff is usually a cry for help. Sometimes young people act up with the youth workers they know will stick around, which is actually a compliment of sorts.

THANK YOU

GOODNIGHT SEE YOU NEXT SHIFT

CAN YOU PLEASE HELP ME

COOKING

DOING CHORES

PLAYING LIKE KIDS

LAUGHING

SMILING

CARING BOUT STAFF

FEELING COMFORTABLE IN TALKING ABOUT THEIR PASTS TO YOU

Chapter 6
Self-care / Change-over / Debriefing / Supervision

Self Care

When working within the youth care industry, self-care is imperative. You can take a self-care quiz at www.myselfcare.org/self.htm. Dennis Portnoy, the licensed psychotherapist who created the quiz, says:

Self-care is not about selfishness or being insensitive to others. It is about making healthy lifestyle choices. Taking care of your-self also involves self-compassion, having clear boundaries, being attuned to your emotional needs and honouring your deepest truth. When you neglect self-care it takes a toll on your health, relationships, effectiveness and you are more susceptible to burnout and compassion fatigue.

Signs and symptoms of excessive job and workplace stress:

» Feeling anxious, irritable, or depressed
» Apathy, loss of interest in work
» Problems sleeping

- » Fatigue
- » Trouble concentrating
- » Muscle tension or headaches
- » Stomach problems
- » Social withdrawal
- » Loss of sex drive
- » Using alcohol or drugs to cope
- » (http://www.helpguide.org/mental/work_stress_management.htm)

Self-care is the most important part of working effectively in most industries. Some people are better equipped for self-care than others. This has been a difficult strategy for me to learn, as I do things to the best of my ability and can be a perfectionist. I tend to take things home and reanalyse the day's events to see if I could have performed my duties in a better way. I say tended, as I have now learned to self-care with several tools. They are:

- » Debrief with others on shift with you
- » Get proper sleep
- » Don't take work home
- » Leave your home life at home
- » Do whatever you like to do to relax
- » Engage in activities not related to work—e.g., gardening, crafts, reading, exercise
- » Eat well

I will share one technique a friend of mine has taught me. When you get home after a not-so-pleasant day, hop in the shower and imagine yourself covered in thick, black coal dust. Let the water run from the top of your head all over your body until you can feel the coal dust coming off and going down the drain. When you get out of the shower, pour a little disinfectant down the drain. Then imagine your body filling with a cool light as you breathe slowly in and out. This may sound crazy—it did to me at first until I tried it. Believe me, you feel so much better after using this technique.

Change-Over

Change-over is a time when the new shift coming on

duty and the staff going off duty exchange the events of the day. The young people can be quite demanding at this time of the day as their world changes once again. You have to remember that we are trying to make a home environment for these children; however, staff come and go on a daily basis, and this can make the children feel anxious.

It is important to explain all the events of the day, as you do not always have time to read the logbook, where daily events or case notes (detailed and factual reports of the day's events) are written down. This change-over information can indicate how the young people may behave and react on your shift.

We have a policy where I am working now to have the first ten minutes of change-over with the young people so that they can share their thoughts of the day. This involves them and will allow staff to talk without the young people wanting immediate attention.

Debriefing

After an incident has occurred, it is most important to debrief:

1: To discuss in order to obtain useful information

2: To carefully review your feelings, what was done during incident, and if anything could have been done better

This means talking to a coordinator or colleague about the incident to let out your feelings, rather than bottle up emotions that you may have experienced during the incident. Bottling up emotions or taking work home can lead to burnout, which can be hazardous to your health and effectiveness in the workplace. This would not be intentional on your part, but it's better to talk out situations so that strategies can be dissected to see what worked and what didn't. Thus, you can develop other approaches.

Supervision

Supervision meetings occur on a regular basis. This is when the coordinator and each staff member meet in private to discuss work for a few hours. During this session, you will review your work and talk about anything that is bothering you. You can also review incidents. The coordinator will ask how you are coping with the young people in your care and if you wish to put forward any ideas. You will also discuss whether you are having any issues with other staff, and the coordinator will give you tools to work these problems out. It is very important to be able to accept constructive conversation. I use the word "conversation" because constructive criticism sounds very negative.

One very important thing to remember: It is just as hard for the young people as it is for you to carry out your caring role successfully.

Transforming Care

There once were children with trauma.
Look after them we oughta.
Their brains were not nurtured,
And their carers are captured
In a world of caring and teaching.
Behaviour is bad, but the child is not mad
Or even bad.
With carer's concern and rapport,
the child will walk out the door,
With life to fulfil,
from carer's teaching a new skill.

This was a poem I wrote after completing transforming care study.

www.ingramcontent.com/pod-product-compliance
Lightning Source LLC
Chambersburg PA
CBHW030540290526
45786CB00004B/1787